My Name Is
HELEN
KELLER

MYRON UHLBERG

illustrated by
JENN KOCSMIERSKY

Albert Whitman & Company
Chicago, Illinois

To Alice Lougee Hagemeyer, foremost graduate of Gallaudet University, who has worked all of her adult life to make libraries more accessible for deaf people; Daniel E. Reynolds, dedicated teacher of braille at the Braille Institute; and Nidya Rojas, who was born blind and has been attending the Braille Institute as a prized student and selfless volunteer—MU

To Jack and Alexis, who teach and inspire me every day—JK

This is a work of biographical fiction. The scenes in this book are based on real events in Helen Keller's life. The lines in italics are Helen's own words.

Library of Congress Cataloging-in-Publication data is on file with the publisher.
Text copyright © 2020 by Myron Ulhberg
Illustrations copyright © 2020 by Jenn Kocsmiersky
First published in the United States of America in 2020 by Albert Whitman & Company
ISBN 978-0-8075-5322-0 (hardcover)
ISBN 978-0-8075-5315-2 (ebook)

Printed in China
10 9 8 7 6 5 4 3 2 1 WKT 24 23 22 21 20

Design by Tim Palin

For more information about Albert Whitman & Company, visit our website at www.albertwhitman.com.

My name is Helen Keller.

This is what I remember.

I see the blue sky.

I hear the wind in the trees.

I say "papa."

One day I got sick. I was hot. I could not swallow.

I slept. And when I woke, my fever was gone. The cool air bathed my skin.

I opened my eyes, and I could not see the blue sky.

I listened, and I could not hear the wind in the trees.

"Mama," I cried.

"Papa," I called, but I could not hear my voice.

I remember these things behind *the veil that clings about my childhood like a golden mist.*

At the age of nineteen months, Helen Keller woke up blind, deaf.

She could no longer see the cows in the fields or the horses who ate apples from her hand.

She could no longer hear the river flow, the birds sing, or the sheep bleat.

It was as if she had been buried alive.

I awoke into *that silent, aimless, dayless life.*

I had my dog, Belle. But I could not hear her happy bark.

I had my doll, Nancy. But I could not see her sweet face.

I stuffed my hands in my mouth, asking for food I would never see.

I clapped my hands. Help me. Help me!

Had anyone heard?

I made up signs.

I shivered for ice cream.

I made slicing signs for bread.

Does anyone understand?

That made me so angry at times that I kicked and screamed until I was exhausted.

I raged.

Light! Give me light!

For five years there was no light.

Then one day, *the light of love shone on me*. My teacher arrived.
It was the third of March, three months before I was seven years old.
My long night was over.

Teacher held my hand under the waterspout of our well.
She spelled W-A-T-E-R into my hand. I did not understand.

Again. And again. And again, she spelled: W-A-T-E-R W-A-T-E-R.

I stood still, my whole attention fixed upon the motions of her fingers.

W-A-T-E-R. Yes! This cold, delicious, wet thing has a name: WATER!

I had now the key to all language.

Ever so slowly, Helen learned. Her mind was a vast, empty well. Her teacher filled it with the water of knowledge.

It seemed more like play than work.

Little Helen learned to spell. She learned new words. She learned to read braille.

Outside the dark prison of my mind was a world filled with things that had a name. Rubbery things that wiggled. Feathery things with wings that beat to be free. Slimy things whose throats bulged in fright. Soft things with pulsating hearts.

Names! Names! I need names for these things. They have no meaning without names.

Give me names!

One day when Helen was eight years old, she went with her younger sister, Mildred, and her teacher, Anne, to gather persimmons. Helen knew the feeling of the word "persimmon" in her hand. Now she could smell them, and she *loved their fragrance.*

She could feel them, hiding in clusters in wet grass under the fallen leaves. And when she held them too tightly, she could taste their sweetness, pooling in her hand.

They went nutting. Helen knew the names Anne signed into her hand: chestnut, hickory nut, walnut. Now, as she felt each hard-textured hull, she could imagine them. And when she crushed them between her fingers, she memorized each peculiar, nutty smell.

"It's time to go home," Teacher said into my hand. "It's late. We'll take a shortcut."

Hand in hand we marched. Soon, the soft grass gave way to the cow path, and I felt the dryness and stones and cow prints. Then I felt something strange under my feet. It felt as if I were *walking on knive*s.

"Where are we?" I asked.

"On the railroad ties," Teacher said. "They're very narrow."

I had to stretch my steps, as the ties were far apart.

Teacher tightened her hold on my hand. "We're on the trestle over the gorge now," she said, almost a whisper in my palm.

I took each step slowly, carefully. Reaching out my foot to the next wooden tie before I let my body follow.

Then I felt it; a tiny shiver of movement ran up my leg. Had I imagined it?

"The train!" Mildred said. "I see the train!"

The rails beneath my feet began to vibrate;
the wooden ties rattled against the loose spikes;
the whole trestle came alive.

Teacher's fingers were insistent, urgent.
"We must get off the track!"

The train roared just inches above our heads. I could feel the vacuum it made as it passed through the still air. I could smell the burning oil, grease, rubber, coal. The fine ash filled my mouth and nose.

The trestle shook, swayed, vibrated, rose, fell. I held on as tightly as I had ever held before. I could feel the train; I sensed its power. And in my mind's eye, I could see the rocks far below. *But I was not afraid.* I had never been so alive.

The train rushed past our heads and was gone. The trestle settled around me.

I would never be afraid of anything.

Helen's well of knowledge continued to fill. She learned of things she could not touch or smell or taste. She learned of love, *and the sweetness that it pours into everything*.

At nineteen, she went to college. Her classmates could see. They could hear. They could speak clearly. Helen could do none of those things. But she could think. She could hope. And she could dream.

And four years later, she graduated with honors. Helen was the first deaf-blind person to have dared to go to college.

I will grow. I will learn.

I will know several languages.

I will read poetry, learn history, write books.

I will meet world leaders. I will stroke the wet mouth of a lion and the quivering back of a tiger.

Where I once knew darkness, I will sense beauty.

Where there was once isolation, I will find the voice of love.

And where the world was once unknowable, it is now filled with possibilities.

Can you see love, touch happiness, taste sorrow, smell joy, hear hope?

Helen knew that *the best and most beautiful things in the world cannot be seen nor even touched*, but are felt in the heart.

As an adult, she traveled the country, meeting people and giving talks. She committed her life to bringing hope and dignity to people with disabilities.

Helen Keller lived in a world of people who could see, and people who could hear. She did not have these abilities. But she had the gift of her mind, coupled with her invincible spirit, and she used them to make the world a better place for everyone.

She died in her sleep one month before her eighty-eighth birthday. But her story lives on, reminding us all that behind every name, there is something precious, waiting to be discovered.

Author's Note

This is a work of biographical fiction. The scenes in this book are based on real events in Helen's life, as detailed in many excellent biographies about Helen Keller: principally *Helen and Teacher* by Joseph P. Lash and *Helen Keller: A Life* by Dorothy Herrmann. I have also relied on Helen's own writings, *The Story of My Life* as well as *Helen Keller's Journal*, and the lines in italics are her words.

In all the thousands of pages written about, and by, Helen Keller, only relatively few devote themselves to the sixty-one months between the age of nineteen months, when she became blind and deaf, and that day in March 1881 when her teacher, Anne Sullivan, came to lead her from darkness into the light. Not surprising, because who could imagine her interior world?

Helen has relatively little to say about those sixty-one months, which she described as "the shadows of the prison house." She did not write *The Story of My Life* until she was an adult. All she could attempt was to try and remember what it was like to be buried in that endless night of solitude and silence. And she referred to that attempt as to "think with a vague remembrance."

My parents also inspire this book. My father, Louis, was the first-born child of hearing immigrant parents. At an early age, he contracted spinal meningitis. When his fever abated, he was totally deaf. My mother, Sarah, was the first-born child of hearing immigrant parents. At an early age, she contracted scarlet fever. When her fever abated, she was totally deaf.

I was the first-born child of these two deaf parents. I could hear.

All my life I have tried to understand what it must have been like for my deaf parents when they were so suddenly rendered deaf as small children.

And as an adult, I have always been fascinated by the story of Helen Keller, who was not only deaf but blind as well. How did my parents cope? How did Helen Keller?

This is a work of imagination based on fact. It is my attempt to discover that truth.

Timeline

1880   Helen Keller is born in Tuscumbia, Alabama, on June 27.

1882   At nineteen months, Helen becomes ill with scarlet fever or meningitis and loses her sight and hearing.

1887   Anne Sullivan, a graduate of the Perkins School for the Blind, is hired to be Helen's tutor. Anne teaches Helen to communicate using manual sign language, a system in which words are spelled one letter at a time, with a different finger position for each letter. In time, Helen also learns to read tactile writing, write by hand in multiple languages, and lip-read by touch. Anne spends the rest of her life, forty-nine years in all, by Helen's side.

1890   At the age of ten, Helen learns to speak, but throughout her life, her speech remains difficult for hearing people to understand.

1900   With Anne as her interpreter, Helen enrolls at Radcliffe College.

1903   Helen's autobiography *The Story of My Life* is released.

1904   Helen graduates with honors from Radcliffe, becoming the first deaf-blind person to earn a bachelor's degree.

1913   Helen travels the country, giving speeches about the challenges she has overcome related to deafness and blindness. Helen's tour helps make her a symbol of self-reliance for all disabled people.

1918   Due in part to Helen's efforts, the United States makes braille the single writing system for the blind.

1924   Helen joins the American Foundation for the Blind and serves as a spokesperson and ambassador. As a result of Helen's work, thirty states create commissions for the blind, rehabilitation centers are built, and education is made more accessible for people with vision loss.

1936   On October 20, Helen's beloved teacher, Anne, dies. Polly Thomson, Helen's longtime secretary, takes over as Helen's interpreter.

1946   Helen goes on her first world tour on behalf of the American Foundation for Overseas Blind. In the next decade, she visits thirty-five countries on five continents, sharing the inspiring story of her life.

1955   Helen wins an Academy Award for a documentary about her life. And she receives an honorary doctoral degree from Harvard University, the first woman to be so honored.

1964   Helen is awarded the US Presidential Medal of Freedom, the nation's highest civilian honor, by President Lyndon Johnson.

1968   On June 1, Helen dies peacefully at her home in Connecticut.

Manual Sign Alphabet

One way Helen and her teacher Anne communicated was by signing words letter by letter into each other's palms. This is the alphabet they used.

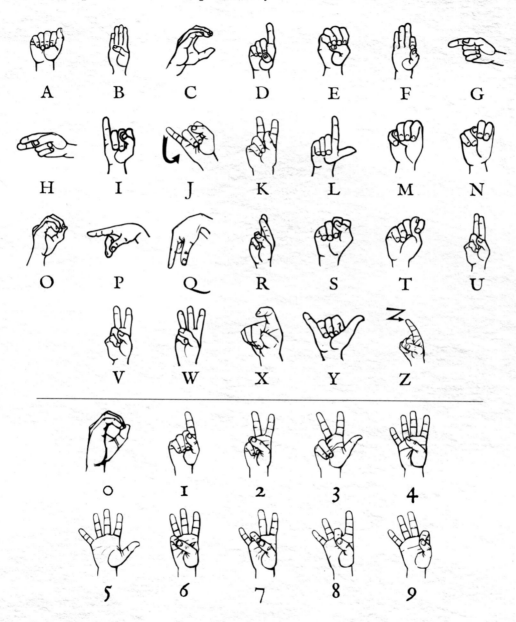

Source Notes

"the veil that clings…": Keller, Helen. *The Story of My Life*, 3. New York: Grosset & Dunlap, 1905.

"that silent, aimless, dayless life": Keller, 13.

"That made me so angry…": Keller, 10.

"Light! Give me light!": Keller, 22.

"the light of love shone on me": Keller, 22.

"I stood still…": Keller, 23.

"I had now the key to all language": Keller, 29.

"It seemed more like play than work": Keller, 34.

"I loved their fragrance": Keller, 53.

"walking on knives": Keller, 54.

"But I was not afraid": Keller, 54.

"and the sweetness that it pours…": Keller, 31.

"the best and most beautiful things…": Keller, 203.